EQUISOCIETY

Manifesto for a Unified Society

Joseph Fansler

MANIFESTO

FOR A UNIFIED SOCIETY

* * *

EQUISOCIETY

3

"Whatever affects one directly, affects all indirectly"
–Martin Luther King Jr.

INTRODUCTION:

In the vast tapestry of human existence, we have witnessed the perils of inequality, the accumulation of wealth, and the monopolization of resources. The EquiSociety envisions a world free from these disparities, creating an egalitarian haven for all.

Core Principles:

1. **Universal Housing**: Every individual has the right to a home. There are no landlords. Homes are provided and maintained by the community for the community.
2. **Egalitarian Work**: All work is valued and recognized equally. Whether you're a teacher, farmer, or engineer, your contribution to society is esteemed at the same level.
3. **Wealth Equilibrium**: The concept of personal wealth accumulation is obsolete. Every resource and product is returned and redistributed for the benefit of all.
4. **Generational Equality**: The notion of passing down excessive wealth or status through generations is removed. Everyone starts with the same opportunities.
5. **Universal Basic Needs**: Food, health, education, and housing are not privileges but basic human rights. They are guaranteed and provided for by the community.

Benefits of EquiSociety:

1. **Reduced Inequality**: With no concentration of wealth, society will see reduced economic disparities.
2. **Promotion of Cooperation**: Without the competition for limited resources, cooperation becomes the norm, fostering a sense of community and mutual respect.

3. **Mental and Physical Well-being**: With basic needs met, individuals can focus on personal growth, creativity, and community building.
4. **Sustainability**: A society without excessive consumption and accumulation promotes environmental sustainability, ensuring that resources are utilized efficiently and responsibly.
5. **End of Poverty**: With resources evenly distributed, the very concept of poverty becomes obsolete.

Conclusion: The EquiSociety is not just a dream; it's a blueprint for a brighter, fairer future. It's a society where every individual, regardless of their background, has an equal shot at a prosperous, fulfilling life. It's a testament to our belief that when we rise as one, we pave the way for a world where everyone can thrive.

Manifesto

FOR A UNIFIED SOCIETY: EQUISOCIETY

Across millennia, human societies have grappled with the challenge of inequality, with systems that allow the few to accumulate at the expense of the many. The vision of EquiSociety is to reimagine this dynamic - a society where no individual is left behind, where resources are not a point of contention but a shared gift. This manifesto offers a journey through the principles and practicalities of such a society, mapping out a future where unity, fairness, and holistic well-being are not mere aspirations but the foundational pillars of our existence.

CHAPTER 1: UNDERSTANDING INEQUALITY

- The Historical Perspective
- Modern Manifestations
- Psychological Impacts
- Economic Consequences
- The Global Picture

CHAPTER 2: THE PHILOSOPHY OF EQUISOCIETY

- Universal Human Rights
- The Spirit of Cooperation
- Redefining Value
- The True Meaning of Wealth
- Sustainability as a Core Tenet

CHAPTER 3: UNIVERSAL HOUSING

- Historical Challenges
- The Vision for Community Housing
- Design and Sustainability
- The Role of Technology
- Long-term Benefits

CHAPTER 4: EGALITARIAN WORK

- The Myth of Job Hierarchy
- Recognizing All Contributions
- The New Age of Collaboration
- Educating for Egalitarian Work
- Addressing Work-Life Balance

CHAPTER 5: WEALTH EQUILIBRIUM

- The Ills of Accumulation
- New Systems of Resource Allocation
- Beyond Money: New Measures of Value
- Celebrating Shared Prosperity
- Challenges and Overcoming Them

CHAPTER 6: GENERATIONAL EQUALITY

- The Legacy of the Past
- Breaking the Chains
- Educating the Future
- The Role of Storytelling
- Celebrating New Traditions

CHAPTER 7: UNIVERSAL BASIC NEEDS

- Redefining Basic Needs
- The Logistics of Universal Access
- Health as a Collective Responsibility
- Nourishing Minds and Bodies
- A Holistic Approach to Well-being

CHAPTER 8: THE ROLE OF TECHNOLOGY

- Historical Technology and Disparity
- Modern Tech as an Equalizer
- Fostering Digital Inclusion
- Ethical Technology
- Visions of a Technological Utopia

CHAPTER 9: CHALLENGES AND CRITIQUES

- Common Misconceptions
- Addressing Valid Concerns
- The Role of Naysayers
- Building Bridges with Doubters
- Continual Learning and Adapting

CHAPTER 10: THE ROAD AHEAD

- Building the First EquiSociety Communities
- Lessons from Other Movements
- The Power of Grassroots Activism
- Global Implications and Adaptations
- A Future of Hope and Unity

Each chapter and subchapter can be fleshed out in greater detail to provide a comprehensive blueprint for the EquiSociety vision.

CHAPTER 1: UNDERSTANDING INEQUALITY

1. The Historical Perspective:

What it is: Inequality has existed in various forms since the dawn of human civilization. From ancient societies where power dynamics were determined by physical strength, lineage, or access to resources, to feudal systems marked by class hierarchies and serfdom, the history of humanity is replete with examples of unequal distributions of power, wealth, and opportunity.

How it works: Historical inequality often arose from a combination of socio-economic structures and cultural norms. For instance, in feudal societies, land ownership was a primary determinant of one's status, leading to a rigid class structure. Similarly, ancient caste systems segmented society based on occupational roles, leading to generations of entrenched inequality.

2. Modern Manifestations:

What it is: While feudal and caste systems might be things of the past in many societies, modern inequality manifests in various ways, from income disparities to gaps in access to education, healthcare, and opportunities.

How it works: Factors like globalization, technology, and policy decisions can either exacerbate or mitigate these gaps. For instance, while technology has made resources and knowledge more accessible to many, it has also led to job obsolescence in certain sectors. Similarly, globalization has led to economic growth but has also often led to a widening gap between the rich and the poor.

3. Psychological Impacts:

What it is: Inequality doesn't just have material consequences; it profoundly impacts mental well-being. Individuals in societies marked by severe disparities can experience feelings of inadequacy, stress, and alienation.

How it works: Humans have an inherent need for fairness and justice. When they perceive that they're getting a raw deal, especially in comparison to others, it can lead to resentment, low self-worth, and increased stress. Furthermore, those at the lower rungs of an unequal society might feel trapped in their circumstances, leading to a sense of hopelessness.

4. Economic Consequences:

What it is: Economic inequality isn't just about numbers; it has real-world implications. A society marked by wide disparities can suffer from reduced economic growth, less social mobility, and even political instability.

How it works: When wealth is concentrated in the hands of a few, it limits consumption and demand at the broader base, which can stifle economic growth. Moreover, when people perceive that hard work doesn't necessarily lead to upward mobility, it can reduce overall societal productivity. Extreme economic disparities can also lead to social unrest, with disenfranchised groups demanding change.

5. The Global Picture:

What it is: Inequality isn't a localized issue; it has a global dimension. Whether we look at disparities between nations in terms of GDP, access to clean water and food, or the digital divide, it's clear that inequality is a global challenge.

How it works: Historical events, like colonization, have left legacies of inequality between countries. Modern phenomena, like international trade policies, can perpetuate these disparities. However, in an interconnected world, these inequalities don't just affect the less fortunate nations. Mass migration, global pandemics, and international conflict are all exacerbated by global inequality.

When one part of the world suffers, the ripple effects can be felt everywhere.

Understanding the roots, manifestations, and consequences of inequality is the first step in envisioning a more equitable future. The lessons of the past and the challenges of the present offer insights into crafting a more just society.

CHAPTER 2: THE PHILOSOPHY OF EQUISOCIETY

1. Universal Human Rights:

What it means: Universal Human Rights emphasize that every individual, irrespective of their race, gender, nationality, or socio-economic background, deserves a set of inalienable rights. These encompass not only political and civil rights but also social, economic, and cultural rights.

Purpose: The core idea behind advocating for Universal Human Rights is to establish a baseline of treatment and opportunities that every person can expect. In the context of EquiSociety, it reinforces the belief that access to basic needs like food, shelter, education, and healthcare isn't a privilege of the few but a right of all.

2. The Spirit of Cooperation:

What it means: Going beyond competition and individualism, the Spirit of Cooperation underscores the importance of working together for collective benefit. It champions the idea that collaborative efforts yield greater results than isolated endeavors.

Purpose: In a world marked by division, the Spirit of Cooperation aims to bridge gaps, foster mutual understanding, and promote shared progress. For EquiSociety, this principle is foundational: resources are pooled, knowledge is shared, and successes are celebrated as a community achievement.

3. Redefining Value:

What it means: In traditional capitalist systems, value is often equated with monetary worth. However, Redefining Value seeks to shift this perspective, considering non-material aspects like community contribution, environmental stewardship, and emotional well-being as equally (if not more) important.

Purpose: By changing our understanding of what is "valuable", society can prioritize actions and systems that promote holistic well-being over mere monetary gain. In EquiSociety, a teacher imparting knowledge or a community member caring for local green spaces would be as valued as an entrepreneur creating a successful start-up.

4. The True Meaning of Wealth:

What it means: Wealth, in many societies, is associated with financial assets. The True Meaning of Wealth broadens this definition to encompass other riches: abundant relationships, access to knowledge, mental and physical well-being, and a clean and thriving environment.

Purpose: In EquiSociety, it's crucial to shift away from the materialistic view of success and prosperity. By expanding the understanding of wealth, society can focus on ensuring everyone has access to these broader riches, leading to a more fulfilling and balanced life for all.

5. Sustainability as a Core Tenet:

What it means: Sustainability emphasizes the need to use resources judiciously, ensuring that they're available for future generations. It's about striking a balance between consumption today and preservation for tomorrow.

Purpose: As EquiSociety seeks to build a world of equal opportunity, it's vital that this vision considers the long-term viability of the planet. Sustainability ensures that as we work towards a more equitable society, we're also being stewards of the environment, ensuring that the Earth remains habitable and bountiful for generations to come.

Rooted in these philosophical principles, EquiSociety envisions a world that is not just fairer but also more holistic, emphasizing the

interconnectedness of individuals, communities, and the
environment.

CHAPTER 3: UNIVERSAL HOUSING

1. Historical Challenges:

Understanding: Throughout history, housing has been a major point of socio-economic contention. From feudal landownership systems, where serfs were tied to lands owned by lords, to the 20th-century housing market bubbles and crises, the right to shelter has often been compromised by economic interests.

Comprehension: The complexities of historical housing systems have led to deeply entrenched inequalities. In many cases, housing was, and still is, viewed purely as an investment or asset, rather than a basic human need. This perspective has, over time, created a landscape where access to decent housing is dictated by wealth, perpetuating cycles of poverty and displacement.

2. The Vision for Community Housing:

Understanding: Community housing in the context of EquiSociety refers to dwellings designed for and by the community, ensuring everyone has a place they can call home, regardless of their economic status.

Comprehension: In this vision, houses are not just structures; they're integral parts of a cohesive community ecosystem. Community housing prioritizes communal spaces, shared resources, and designs that foster interaction and mutual support among residents. It dismantles the traditional landlord-tenant dynamic, focusing instead on collective ownership or stewardship.

3. Design and Sustainability:

Understanding: To make universal housing a reality, it's vital to consider not only the quantity but also the quality of homes. This means adopting designs that are both functional and sustainable, ensuring they're built to last and have minimal environmental impact.

Comprehension: Sustainable design incorporates local materials, energy-efficient structures, and green technologies. It's about creating homes that are in harmony with their environment, reducing waste, energy consumption, and carbon footprint. Furthermore, in the EquiSociety vision, designs would be adaptable to different environments and cultural contexts.

4. The Role of Technology:

Understanding: Technology offers tools and innovations that can revolutionize the way we approach housing, from construction methods to resource management.

Comprehension: Modern technology can be harnessed to create smart homes that optimize energy use, manage waste efficiently, and even produce their own renewable energy. Furthermore, advancements in construction technology, such as 3D printing, can significantly reduce building costs and time. In a universal housing model, technology would be leveraged to ensure homes are not only widely accessible but also future-proof and environmentally friendly.

5. Long-term Benefits:

Understanding: Universal housing isn't just about putting roofs over heads. It carries a multitude of long-term benefits for individuals, communities, and societies at large.

Comprehension: With secure housing, individuals experience improved mental and physical well-being, leading to increased productivity and reduced healthcare costs. Stable housing can also improve educational outcomes for children. At the community level, universal housing fosters stronger social bonds, reducing crime and social unrest. Economically, when people aren't burdened by exorbitant housing costs, they can invest in other areas, spurring broader economic growth and innovation.

In sum, the Universal Housing vision of EquiSociety is about reimagining the very foundation of our living spaces. It champions the idea that everyone deserves not just a house, but a sustainable, technologically advanced, and community-centric home.

CHAPTER 4: EGALITARIAN WORK

1. The Myth of Job Hierarchy:

Understanding: Job hierarchy traditionally categorizes occupations based on perceived importance, prestige, or economic compensation. Such a hierarchical approach often places professions like CEOs, doctors, or lawyers at the top, while undervaluing roles in care work, sanitation, or agriculture.

Benefits and Purpose: By debunking the myth of job hierarchy, society can cultivate a more inclusive and holistic understanding of work. Every job plays a crucial role in the intricate web of societal functions. Recognizing this promotes respect across professions, ensures fair compensation, and counters systemic prejudices and biases in the job market.

2. Recognizing All Contributions:

Understanding: Beyond formal employment, countless contributions are made daily that don't fit into traditional economic models—like homemaking, community service, or volunteer work.

Benefits and Purpose: Recognizing all contributions means acknowledging the value of these often-invisible efforts. By doing so, EquiSociety would foster a culture where individuals feel seen and appreciated for their roles, regardless of economic compensation. This not only boosts societal morale but can also influence policies that support such contributions, like stipends for caregivers or community organizers.

3. The New Age of Collaboration:

Understanding: Historically, many work environments have emphasized competition over collaboration. However, in an egalitarian work setting, the emphasis shifts towards teamwork, shared goals, and mutual success.

Benefits and Purpose: Collaborative work environments can lead to improved problem-solving, increased innovation, and a more cohesive work culture. When individuals come together, pooling their diverse skills and perspectives, the results are often more robust and multifaceted than solo endeavors. For EquiSociety, promoting collaboration ensures that the collective intelligence of the community drives progress.

4. Educating for Egalitarian Work:

Understanding: Traditional education systems often perpetuate job hierarchies, guiding students towards "prestigious" roles and overlooking other vital professions.

Benefits and Purpose: Reforming education to emphasize the value of all types of work ensures a more balanced and prepared workforce. It encourages students to pursue passions rather than mere prestige, leading to a more fulfilled and motivated workforce. Furthermore, it can reduce skills shortages in undervalued yet essential sectors.

5. Addressing Work-Life Balance:

Understanding: In many contemporary societies, work often overshadows other aspects of life, leading to burnout, stress, and reduced family or leisure time.

Benefits and Purpose: Promoting work-life balance in an egalitarian work model means recognizing the importance of rest, leisure, and personal pursuits. Such a balance not only enhances individual well-being but also boosts productivity and creativity when individuals are working. It sends a message that while work is important, it is just one facet of a multifaceted human life.

Egalitarian Work, as proposed by EquiSociety, isn't just about redefining roles and compensation. It's a profound shift in how society perceives, values, and engages with work—ensuring that every individual feels valued, fulfilled, and balanced in their professional endeavors.

CHAPTER 5: WEALTH EQUILIBRIUM

1. The Ills of Accumulation:

Understanding: Historically, accumulation of wealth by a select few has been seen as a marker of success and power. However, when vast wealth accumulates in the hands of a minority, it can lead to socio-economic disparities, reduced opportunities for the majority, and societal unrest.

Reason and Purpose: Addressing the problems associated with excessive wealth accumulation allows for a more equitable distribution of resources. In doing so, EquiSociety aims to prevent the concentration of power, reduce wealth-driven inequalities, and ensure that resources are used for the betterment of all, rather than the luxury of a few.

2. New Systems of Resource Allocation:

Understanding: Traditional economic systems often prioritize capital accumulation, profit motives, and individual wealth. In contrast, new systems of resource allocation would prioritize collective well-being, sustainability, and equitable access.

Reason and Purpose: By adopting new allocation systems, EquiSociety seeks to ensure that resources—be it food, housing, education, or technology—are distributed based on need and communal benefit rather than purchasing power. This shift is vital in creating a society where everyone has access to the tools and resources they need to thrive.

3. Beyond Money: New Measures of Value:

Understanding: While money has been the predominant measure of value in most societies, there's a growing recognition that true value encompasses more than just financial worth. Other aspects, such as well-being, environmental health, and community cohesion, are equally crucial.

Reason and Purpose: Introducing new measures of value means expanding society's understanding of success and prosperity. EquiSociety believes that by valuing non-monetary aspects of life, we can foster a richer, more holistic society where success is not just about individual wealth but also about communal health, happiness, and harmony.

4. Celebrating Shared Prosperity:

Understanding: Shared prosperity refers to a society in which progress benefits all members, not just a privileged few. It's a scenario where economic growth translates into improved living standards for everyone.

Reason and Purpose: By celebrating shared prosperity, EquiSociety aims to shift cultural narratives away from individualistic triumphs towards communal achievements. Recognizing and lauding collective progress fosters a sense of unity, reduces feelings of envy or competition, and strengthens societal bonds.

5. Challenges and Overcoming Them:

Understanding: Achieving wealth equilibrium is no easy feat. It requires dismantling entrenched systems, addressing cultural beliefs about wealth, and navigating potential resistance from those who benefit from the status quo.

Reason and Purpose: Acknowledging these challenges is crucial for transparency and preparation. By proactively identifying potential hurdles, EquiSociety can develop strategies to address them. This might involve educational campaigns, policy reforms, or community dialogues. The purpose is to ensure that the journey towards wealth equilibrium is inclusive, deliberate, and considerate of diverse perspectives.

In essence, Wealth Equilibrium in the EquiSociety framework isn't just about equal distribution of assets. It's about redefining success, value, and prosperity in a way that emphasizes collective well-being, equitable opportunities, and the holistic richness of society.

CHAPTER 6: GENERATIONAL EQUALITY

1. The Legacy of the Past:

Understanding: Every generation inherits certain legacies—both tangible and intangible. This includes wealth, traditions, beliefs, prejudices, and debts. Some of these legacies can perpetuate inequalities, while others can be sources of strength and wisdom.

Comprehensive Look: Generational equality requires an honest examination of what's being handed down. This includes acknowledging both the positive contributions and the problematic aspects. The inherited systems of discrimination, bias, or environmental degradation, for example, are aspects that future generations should not have to shoulder. EquiSociety proposes a critical analysis of our inherited legacies to determine which ones foster equality and which ones perpetuate division.

2. Breaking the Chains:

Understanding: Historical injustices, long-standing prejudices, and accumulated wealth disparities can tether future generations to a past that doesn't serve them.

Comprehensive Look: "Breaking the chains" involves active efforts to dismantle systemic issues that perpetuate generational inequalities. This could mean reparative measures for historical wrongs, economic policies that prevent the hoarding of wealth within families over generations, and societal norms that challenge rather than uphold outdated prejudices. The goal is to ensure every generation has an equal starting point, free from the burdens of the past.

3. Educating the Future:

Understanding: Education plays a pivotal role in shaping the mindsets and opportunities of new generations. It's not just about academia, but also the values, worldviews, and skills we impart.

Comprehensive Look: For generational equality, education needs a paradigm shift. This involves curricula that prioritize inclusivity, critical thinking, and global citizenship. It's about nurturing a generation that's conscious of its past, active in its present, and visionary about its future. EquiSociety envisions an education system where knowledge isn't just about personal advancement but also societal betterment.

4. The Role of Storytelling:

Understanding: Stories have the power to shape perceptions, beliefs, and identities. Through stories, histories are remembered, values are imparted, and visions for the future are crafted.

Comprehensive Look: In the context of generational equality, storytelling can be a tool for both reflection and projection. By retelling histories honestly, including the voices of the marginalized, societies can heal from past wounds and ensure they aren't repeated. Similarly, stories that envision an equitable future can inspire change and guide collective actions. Storytelling, in various forms like literature, media, or oral traditions, becomes a bridge between generations, conveying lessons, dreams, and aspirations.

5. Celebrating New Traditions:

Understanding: Traditions are the glue that binds communities across time. While many traditions are sources of joy and identity, some can perpetuate outdated beliefs or practices.

Comprehensive Look: EquiSociety promotes the idea of evolving traditions. This means holding onto the core essence of traditions that unify and uplift, while being open to modifying or shedding practices that no longer align with the values of equality. Celebrating new traditions involves recognizing the dynamic nature of culture and embracing changes that reflect the evolving understanding of justice, equality, and community.

Generational Equality, as envisioned by EquiSociety, is not about erasing the past, but about learning from it, healing where needed, and crafting a future where every generation has the tools, knowledge, and freedom to create a better world for the next. It's a commitment to ongoing growth, understanding, and shared responsibility.

CHAPTER 7: UNIVERSAL BASIC NEEDS

1. Redefining Basic Needs:

Understanding: Traditionally, basic needs have been identified as food, water, shelter, and clothing. However, in the context of a progressive society, this definition needs expansion to include aspects like healthcare, education, mental well-being, and access to information.

Approach and Solutions: To redefine basic needs, a comprehensive assessment of what constitutes a fulfilling and dignified life in modern society is necessary. Engaging community dialogues, sociological research, and interdisciplinary collaboration can help formulate a broader list of universal needs. Policies can then be crafted to prioritize and address these needs systematically.

2. The Logistics of Universal Access:

Understanding: Ensuring everyone has access to their basic needs is a complex logistical challenge. It involves infrastructure, resource allocation, and systems that can adapt to changing demands and circumstances.

Approach and Solutions: The first step is a detailed mapping of resources, both existing and required. Technologies like blockchain could track resource distribution with transparency. Collaborations between public, private, and community sectors can optimize resource management. Modular and scalable solutions, such as mobile clinics or digital education hubs, can be designed to ensure flexibility and reach to even the most remote communities.

3. Health as a Collective Responsibility:

Understanding: Health isn't just an individual concern; it impacts communities, economies, and societies. Disease outbreaks, for instance, can have ramifications beyond affected individuals.

Approach and Solutions: Adopting a collective approach means integrating health awareness and practices into daily life and societal systems. This could involve public health campaigns, community health programs, and the incorporation of health education from early schooling. Additionally, investing in preventive care, accessible medical facilities, and research can ensure a healthier society, reducing the long-term burdens on healthcare systems.

4. Nourishing Minds and Bodies:

Understanding: Nutrition plays a pivotal role in overall well-being. However, it's not just about physical sustenance. Intellectual and emotional nourishment, through education, arts, and positive social interactions, is equally vital.

Approach and Solutions: A dual strategy is essential here. On the physical front, policies promoting sustainable agriculture, reducing food wastage, and ensuring balanced diets are crucial. This might involve community farming projects, nutritional education, and food distribution networks. On the intellectual and emotional front, investing in comprehensive education, promoting cultural and arts programs, and creating inclusive social spaces can ensure holistic nourishment.

5. A Holistic Approach to Well-being:

Understanding: Well-being is multi-dimensional, encompassing physical health, mental health, social connections, and purposeful living.

Approach and Solutions: A holistic approach would integrate the various facets of well-being into societal structures. This might involve:

- Mental health initiatives in workplaces and schools.

- Spaces for community interactions and support.
- Programs that allow individuals to pursue passions and skills beyond their professional roles.
- Sustainable practices that align with environmental well-being.

In essence, Universal Basic Needs in the EquiSociety model go beyond mere survival. The focus is on creating an environment where every individual doesn't just exist but thrives, with access to all the tools and resources that ensure a holistic, dignified, and purposeful life.

CHAPTER 8: THE ROLE OF TECHNOLOGY

1. Historical Technology and Disparity:

Description: Historically, technological advancements have been a double-edged sword. While they brought about revolutions in industry, communication, and health, they also often resulted in socio-economic disparities. Those who controlled or had access to new technology garnered power, wealth, and influence, leaving behind those who didn't. The industrial revolution, for instance, while revolutionizing manufacturing, also exacerbated class divides and labor exploitation.

Purpose: By understanding the historical implications of technology, we can become more aware of its potential pitfalls. Recognizing past mistakes ensures that as we advance, we do so with inclusivity and foresight, avoiding the repetition of creating technological disparities.

2. Modern Tech as an Equalizer:

Description: In today's digital age, technology has the potential to level the playing field like never before. From online education platforms that offer learning to anyone with an internet connection, to apps that bridge language barriers, modern tech holds the promise of inclusivity.

Purpose: This section underscores the transformational potential of technology in promoting equality. By highlighting successful examples and case studies, it aims to inspire more innovations that directly address societal imbalances and empower marginalized communities.

3. Fostering Digital Inclusion:

Description: Digital inclusion refers to the effort to ensure everyone, regardless of socio-economic status, disability, age, or geography, has equal access to modern ICT (Information and Communication Technologies) and the skills to use them effectively.

Purpose: Promoting digital inclusion is essential for a society aiming for holistic equality. This section will outline strategies like building robust IT infrastructures in remote areas, offering digital literacy programs, and ensuring that technology is accessible to people with disabilities. The aim is to ensure no one is left behind in the digital age.

4. Ethical Technology:

Description: As technology continues to permeate every facet of human life, ethical considerations become paramount. This includes issues of privacy, data security, artificial intelligence decision-making, and the environmental impact of tech industries.

Purpose: Highlighting the importance of ethical technology serves as a reminder that while advancements are beneficial, they must always be aligned with human rights, environmental sustainability, and societal well-being. This section will delve into best practices, challenges, and potential regulations to ensure technology serves humanity and not the other way around.

5. Visions of a Technological Utopia:

Description: A technological utopia envisions a future where technology, in harmony with nature and society, creates an environment of abundance, well-being, and interconnectedness. It's a world where AI, robotics, virtual reality, and more are integrated seamlessly, amplifying human potential and ensuring equitable access to resources and opportunities.

Purpose: Painting a vision of a technological utopia serves as an aspirational goal. By defining what an ideal tech-integrated society looks like, stakeholders—be it innovators, policymakers, or the general public—can work collaboratively towards it. It's a beacon of hope and a roadmap to a future where technology truly uplifts every individual.

In essence, "The Role of Technology" in the EquiSociety framework is to emphasize technology's vast potential to be a catalyst for societal change, while also ensuring it remains a tool for empowerment and not exploitation. It's about harnessing the power of innovation while staying grounded in ethical and equitable practices.

CHAPTER 9:
CHALLENGES AND
CRITIQUES

1. Common Misconceptions:

Description: As with any transformative idea, misconceptions can arise, often born from misinformation, misunderstanding, or fear of the unknown. For EquiSociety, misconceptions might include beliefs like "equality means everyone is the same" or "this is just a veiled attempt at communism."

Understanding: It's crucial to identify these misconceptions early on and address them head-on. By clarifying what EquiSociety truly stands for and providing clear distinctions from other ideologies or systems, we can ensure that the movement's core principles are understood and not misrepresented.

2. Addressing Valid Concerns:

Description: Constructive criticism and genuine concerns are different from misconceptions. These might revolve around the feasibility of certain ideas, potential economic implications, or concerns about personal freedoms and autonomy.

Understanding: Taking these concerns seriously is key to refining and improving the EquiSociety framework. By engaging in open dialogue, considering empirical evidence, and revisiting certain principles if necessary, we can address and assuage these valid concerns, thereby strengthening the movement's foundation.

3. The Role of Naysayers:

Description: In every movement, there will be naysayers – those who oppose the idea, often vocally, regardless of the amount of information provided. Their opposition might be rooted in personal gain, ideological differences, or simply a resistance to change.

Understanding: Recognizing the role of naysayers is vital. Instead of seeing them purely as obstacles, they can be viewed as individuals who challenge the movement to better itself. Their criticisms, even if rooted in bias, can offer insights into areas of potential vulnerability or blind spots within the EquiSociety framework.

4. Building Bridges with Doubters:

Description: Doubters differ from naysayers in that their skepticism isn't absolute. They might be on the fence or require more information, experiences, or reassurances before they align with the movement.

Understanding: Engaging with doubters is a pivotal strategy for EquiSociety. By creating platforms for dialogue, fostering community engagement, and showcasing real-world examples of EquiSociety principles in action, we can bridge the gap between doubt and belief. These efforts are about creating an inclusive environment where questions are welcomed, and clarity is sought.

5. Continual Learning and Adapting:

Description: The world is dynamic, and societal needs, challenges, and tools are ever-evolving. As such, no movement or ideology can remain static.

Understanding: EquiSociety must embrace a culture of perpetual learning and adaptation. By staying attuned to global shifts, technological advancements, and emerging societal needs, the movement can ensure it remains relevant, effective, and aligned with its core mission. This also means being receptive to feedback, both internal and external, and being willing to iterate and evolve based on that feedback.

In essence, "Challenges and Critiques" serves as a mirror for EquiSociety. By reflecting on external perceptions, criticisms, and feedback, the movement can engage in self-assessment, growth, and refinement. This chapter underscores the importance of humility, openness, and resilience in the face of challenges, ensuring EquiSociety remains a robust and evolving force for societal betterment.

CHAPTER 10: THE ROAD AHEAD

1. Building the First EquiSociety Communities:

Description: The journey towards a globally accepted EquiSociety begins at the local level. These initial communities will serve as living laboratories, embodying the principles of EquiSociety in real-world settings.

Vision: The establishment of pilot EquiSociety communities will prioritize inclusivity, sustainability, and shared prosperity. From housing and resource allocation to community-driven decision-making, these hubs will showcase the tangible benefits of the EquiSociety model. They will serve as inspirations, their successes and challenges providing invaluable lessons for broader implementation.

2. Lessons from Other Movements:

Description: Historically, many movements have sought social change, justice, and equality. These movements, from civil rights to environmental advocacy, offer a wealth of insights.

Vision: By studying past movements, EquiSociety can glean lessons on strategies, pitfalls, resilience, and mobilization. These historical precedents can act as guideposts, ensuring the movement is informed by the successes and failures of those who paved the way for societal change.

3. The Power of Grassroots Activism:

Description: Real change often emanates from the ground up. Grassroots activism involves local individuals advocating for change in their communities, using local knowledge and connections to galvanize support.

Vision: EquiSociety will harness the energy and authenticity of grassroots activism. By empowering individuals to take ownership of the movement in their locales, a genuine, organic momentum can be built. From community workshops to localized campaigns, grassroots efforts will be the beating heart of the EquiSociety movement.

4. Global Implications and Adaptations:

Description: While the principles of EquiSociety are universal, their application might differ based on regional, cultural, and socio-economic contexts.

Vision: As EquiSociety expands globally, it will prioritize adaptability and respect for local nuances. Collaborative engagements with local leaders, understanding regional challenges, and adapting strategies accordingly will be crucial. This ensures that the movement, while rooted in universal principles, remains flexible and relevant across diverse global contexts.

5. A Future of Hope and Unity:

Description: At its core, EquiSociety is more than just a set of principles or policies—it's a vision of a future where every individual is valued, where the collective good takes precedence over individualistic excess, and where unity and shared purpose drive progress.

Vision: The road ahead envisions a world where differences are celebrated, where access to basic needs isn't a privilege but a right, and where the collective spirit of humanity thrives. It's a world where generations look back with gratitude, knowing their predecessors chose unity over division, hope over despair, and love over indifference.

In conclusion, "The Road Ahead" paints a picture of the EquiSociety journey—filled with challenges, adaptations, and unwavering commitment. This chapter is both a roadmap and a beacon, guiding proponents of the movement towards a brighter, equitable, and harmonious future. It's a call to action, a promise of perseverance, and a testament to the indomitable human spirit that seeks a better world for all.

Creating an equitable society as outlined in the EquiSociety framework is no small feat. It requires meticulous planning, widespread mobilization, and long-term commitment. Here's a detailed plan of execution:

1. Awareness and Education:

- **Objective**: Educate the public about the EquiSociety vision, its benefits, and how it addresses current societal flaws.
- **Actions**:
  - Develop educational materials: brochures, documentaries, online courses, and workshops.
  - Partner with educational institutions to introduce curriculum components about EquiSociety principles.
  - Organize public seminars, webinars, and community gatherings.

2. Grassroots Mobilization:

- **Objective**: Build a strong foundation at the local level, rallying community support.
- **Actions**:
  - Identify and train community leaders or champions.
  - Organize community projects or initiatives that showcase EquiSociety principles in action.
  - Engage in community dialogue sessions, town hall meetings, and feedback loops.

3. Establish Pilot Communities:

- **Objective**: Test the feasibility and benefits of the EquiSociety model in real-world settings.
- **Actions**:
  - Identify suitable locations based on various criteria like population density, resources, and local support.

- Collaborate with urban planners, sociologists, and local communities to design these pilot hubs.
- Monitor, evaluate, and regularly iterate based on findings.

4. Legislative and Policy Advocacy:

- **Objective**: Influence policy decisions to support the EquiSociety vision.
- **Actions**:
    - Collaborate with legal experts to draft policy proposals.
    - Lobby with policymakers, illustrating the societal benefits of adopting EquiSociety principles.
    - Encourage public advocacy campaigns to create demand for policy changes.

5. Technological Partnerships:

- **Objective**: Ensure technology acts as an enabler and equalizer in the EquiSociety framework.
- **Actions**:
    - Partner with tech firms to develop tools promoting digital inclusivity, ethical tech, and resource allocation.
    - Foster research and development in sustainable and equitable tech solutions.
    - Host hackathons or innovation challenges focusing on EquiSociety challenges.

6. Financial Structuring:

- **Objective**: Secure funding and develop economic models that align with EquiSociety principles.
- **Actions**:
    - Source funding through grants, philanthropy, and impact investments.
    - Design financial models that prioritize collective well-being over excessive accumulation.

- Collaborate with economists to continually refine these models, ensuring sustainability and resilience.

7. Cultural and Social Integration:

- **Objective**: Ensure cultural and social norms evolve in tandem with EquiSociety values.
- **Actions**:
    - Promote art, literature, music, and media that reflect EquiSociety principles.
    - Encourage intercultural dialogues, fostering respect and understanding.
    - Celebrate successes and milestones, building a shared sense of pride and identity.

8. Continuous Evaluation and Iteration:

- **Objective**: Ensure the movement remains relevant, effective, and responsive to societal needs.
- **Actions**:
    - Establish research partnerships with universities and think tanks.
    - Conduct regular surveys, feedback sessions, and impact assessments.
    - Organize annual conventions or forums to discuss findings, challenges, and future directions.

9. Global Outreach and Expansion:

- **Objective**: Scale the EquiSociety model globally, adapting to various cultural and regional contexts.
- **Actions**:
    - Build partnerships with international NGOs, governments, and institutions.
    - Train global ambassadors to introduce the EquiSociety framework in diverse settings.
    - Share resources, learnings, and best practices across borders.

10. Resilience and Longevity Planning:

- **Objective**: Ensure the EquiSociety movement remains robust, adaptive, and enduring.
- **Actions**:
    - Develop contingency plans for potential challenges or crises.
    - Foster a culture of adaptability, innovation, and learning within the movement.
    - Engage younger generations, ensuring continuity and fresh perspectives.

In essence, executing the EquiSociety vision is a holistic endeavor, encompassing education, community building, policy advocacy, technological innovation, and global outreach. With dedication, collaboration, and a clear roadmap, the dream of an equitable society can become a tangible reality.

THE IMPERATIVE OF EQUISOCIETY FOR HUMANITY:

A Summary

In an age marked by unprecedented technological advances, global interconnectedness, and vast resources, stark contrasts of inequality, ecological degradation, and societal fragmentation also cast a profound shadow. The importance of transitioning towards an equitable society – the EquiSociety – is underscored by several critical imperatives.

Firstly, **societal harmony and stability** are at stake. History has repeatedly demonstrated that extreme disparities, whether in wealth, access to resources, or opportunities, breed discontent, unrest, and often, upheaval. An equitable society reduces such tensions, fostering an environment where each individual feels valued, heard, and protected.

Second, **human potential** is universally distributed, but opportunity is not. The EquiSociety seeks to rectify this misalignment. By ensuring every individual, regardless of birth circumstances, has the tools and opportunities to fulfill their potential, humanity as a whole stands to benefit from a vast reservoir of untapped talent, innovation, and creativity.

Moreover, the **environmental imperative** cannot be overlooked. A society that prioritizes collective welfare over unbridled consumption is more likely to adopt sustainable practices, recognizing that the health of our planet and its inhabitants are intricately linked. The EquiSociety ethos inherently champions a balanced coexistence with nature, ensuring a viable world for future generations.

From a **psychological perspective**, the strains of living in a deeply unequal society manifest in myriad ways: mental health challenges, feelings of alienation, and a pervasive sense of insecurity. The EquiSociety promises a world where well-being is holistic, considering not just physical, but also mental, emotional, and social health.

Lastly, the **moral and ethical case** for EquiSociety is profound. If humanity prides itself on its progress, its cultures, and its moral evolution, then it is incumbent upon us to create a world where justice, fairness, and dignity are not just ideals but lived realities.

In conclusion, the push towards EquiSociety is not merely a choice; it's an imperative. For the sake of societal cohesion, the realization of human potential, environmental sustainability, holistic well-being, and our collective moral compass, the vision of a balanced, just, and harmonious world is one we must tirelessly pursue. The promise of EquiSociety is not just a better world, but a humanity truly realized.

THE GLOBAL CONTINUITY IMPERATIVE:

An EquiSociety Founded on Earth-First Principles

The paradigm shift towards an EquiSociety is not merely an aspiration for human equity; it is intricately bound with the imperative of global continuity and an unwavering Earth-first approach. In this envisioned society, every decision, initiative, and action is harmoniously tethered to the well-being of our planet and all life forms that inhabit it.

Central to this is the recognition of our planet's fragile ecosystems, where every species, every waterway, and every forest plays a crucial role in the intricate web of life. By prioritizing global continuity, the EquiSociety inherently advocates for practices and philosophies that ensure the sustainable coexistence of all life forms.

Ownership, especially of land and natural resources, has historically been a root cause of exploitation, conflict, and environmental degradation. In the EquiSociety framework, this concept undergoes a radical transformation. Land isn't "owned" in the traditional sense; instead, it's stewarded. Every individual, community, and nation becomes a caretaker, ensuring that the land is used sustainably, respectfully, and equitably. This philosophy extends to the very riches of the Earth – water, minerals, flora, and fauna. They aren't commodities to be claimed or hoarded but shared gifts to be used judiciously for the collective benefit.

This Earth-first approach also underscores the interconnectedness of our global community. In the EquiSociety, borders are not barriers but reminders of our diverse landscapes and cultures. The health of a forest in South America impacts the air quality in Asia; the preservation of polar ice caps affects coastlines thousands of miles away. This profound interdependence mandates global collaboration, shared responsibility, and a united effort towards ecological restoration and preservation.

Moreover, it's essential to instill this global continuity ethos at the grassroots level. Education, storytelling, and cultural practices will play pivotal roles in fostering a deep-seated reverence for the Earth. Future generations will grow up understanding their role as stewards, ensuring that the Earth-first principle becomes an intrinsic part of human identity.

In summary, the EquiSociety vision is not solely about human equity; it's about redefining our relationship with the Earth, ensuring that every decision prioritizes the planet's health and the continuity of all its inhabitants. It's a call for a symbiotic existence, where humanity thrives not at the expense of the Earth but in harmonious partnership with it. This holistic, Earth-first approach is not just an essential component of the EquiSociety; it's the very foundation upon which it stands.